My First Bible Words

A Kid's Devotional

Presented to

---

by

---

occasion

---

date

---

*Dedicated to all the children
and grandchildren of the world.*

My First
Bible
Words
• A Kid's Devotional •

William O. Noller
& Kenneth N. Taylor

Illustrations by
Corbert Gauthier
Richard Hook and Frances Hook

CANDLE
BOOKS

Other Candle Books by Kenneth N.Taylor:
My First Bible in Pictures
My Little Bible in Pictures

Worldwide co-editions organised and produced by Angus
Hudson Ltd, Concorde House, Grenville Place, Mill Hill,
London NW7 3SA
Tel: Int +44 20 8959 3668 Fax: Int +44 20 8959 3678

Published by Candle Books 2000.
Distributed by STL,
PO Box 300,
Carlisle,
Cumbria CA3 0QS

ISBN 1 85985 256 4

Printed in Singapore

Contents

Dear Parent — *also Grandparents, Aunts, and Uncles!*

This book is a way to introduce your child to words that explain the great truths of the Bible and our Christian faith.

This is not a Bible storybook but a Bible word book of short devotions and teachings, each based on one Bible word. The book explains what each word means and how it relates to your child. It does this in simple sentences that young children can understand and enjoy.

Let us further explain the difference between this book and a Bible storybook: A Bible storybook may tell about Jesus walking on the water on the Sea of Galilee. My First Bible Words explains that what Jesus did was a miracle and that Jesus could do it because he is God's Son. A Bible storybook may also tell about Jesus at the Temple in Jerusalem when he was twelve years old. My First Bible Words tells what the Temple was—a special place to worship God. It also tells what the word worship means, and it explains that your child should worship our Lord. So this little book is full of Bible teaching as well as definitions of Bible words.

You will be able to help your children understand what it means to believe, trust, forgive, and witness. And you can help them by means of this book to understand essential Christian themes, such as the Bible, God, Jesus, sin, salvation, Christian living, and the church. Everything in the Apostles' Creed is treated here.

May God the Holy Spirit use this book to direct many young hearts toward understanding spiritual truth. May he do this as he enlightens their minds about the Bible's words.

William O. Noller
Kenneth N. Taylor

The Bible

Special names for God's Book

Bible

The word Bible means "books." There are many books in the Bible. All together they make one very special book—God's book. In the Bible, God tells us about himself. He tells us that he loves us very much, and he tells us how we should live.

We can learn all about God and his love in the Bible. God says we should look through the Bible—to read it and learn about him (Isaiah 34:16).

Why is the Bible such a special book?

Thank you, God, for your special book,
the Bible. I'm glad you tell me in your
book that you love me. Amen.

Word

The Bible is filled with God's words. So we call the Bible the Word, or God's Word, or the Word of God. In it God talks to you and tells you what he wants you to know.

In God's Word one of the things God tells you is that he is "always ready to help in times of trouble" (Psalm 46:1).

Hold a Bible in your hands. Look at it and open it. This book you are holding is filled with God's words.

*T*hank you, dear God, for telling me many good
things in your Word, the Bible. Amen.

Scripture

Do you remember that sometimes we call the Bible *God's Word?* Another name for the Bible is Scripture, which means "the writings." When we talk about Scripture, we mean the writing of God. All of the Bible is written by God.

The Bible is like a letter from God. It is written to all his people. It is written to you.

What does the word *Scripture* mean?

*D*ear God, I really like Bible stories.
I'm glad that all Scripture was written by you.
Thank you for writing it to me. Amen.

The Bible

What should we know
about the Bible

God

The Bible tells me about God. I can listen to Bible stories and learn about God. I can learn that God has always lived. No one lived before him. The Bible also tells me that God loves me very much and wants me to be happy and good.

I'm glad that the Bible teaches me about God. He can be my best friend, so I want to know him better and better!

What are two things the Bible tells us about God?

*T*hank you, dear God, for all the things I can learn about you in the Bible.

true

The Bible is true. That means we can believe everything it says. We can believe the Bible because God gave it to us. God wants us to listen to the Bible, believe that it is true, and obey it.

Did you ever hear anyone say, "That's not true; I don't believe that"? But everything the Bible tells us is true. We can believe whatever it says.

What book tells us only the truth?

*L*ord God, I'm so glad that I can believe
everything the Bible says.

scribes

In Bible times there were no printing presses to make Bibles. Every word was copied by hand. The men who copied the Bible were called scribes.

Bible people knew that God's Word was important. So scribes copied it, one word at a time.

Your mother can be a scribe and print these words for you: God loves me. How long do you think it would take your mother to write all the words in the Bible, like the scribes did?

*D*ear God, thank you that I can have
my very own copy of your Bible!
In Jesus' name. Amen.

scrolls

Bible people did not have books. Words were written on scrolls. These were like long sheets of paper that were rolled up. Scribes wrote God's words on Bible scrolls.

God helped to keep the Bible scrolls safe. Now we have the words from those scrolls in our Bibles!

Ask someone to print your favourite Bible verse on a sheet of paper. Then roll it up to look like a scroll.

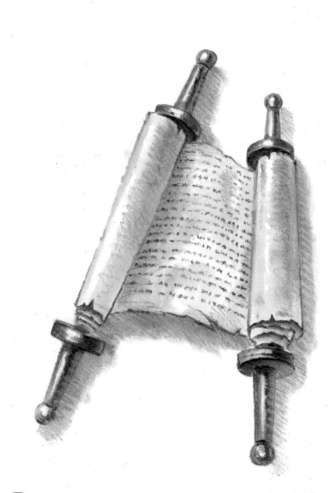

*D*ear God, thank you for machines that print Bibles
quickly. Now everyone can have a Bible.
Thank you for my Bible or my Bible word book.

forever

Forever is always. God's Word, the Bible, will last forever. We will always have God's words to help us know what is right. We will always have God's words to help us know about his love.

God's words were here when your great-grandparents were children. God's words will still be here when you grow up and have children. His words will never get old.

How long will we have God's words?

*L*ord, I thank you for promising that
your words, which are in the Bible,
will be true forever. Amen.

The Bible

What is in the Bible?

history

The story of how people lived long ago is called history. The Bible has the history of God's people in it. God wants people to know about himself. So he wrote about people like Abraham and Sarah to help us know how much he loves us and how much we can love him.

Your mum and dad can tell you about what they did when they were kids. The Bible tells what people did a long time before that.

What can you learn about God from God's people?

*T*hank you, dear God, for Bible stories.
I know they happened a long time ago,
but you want me to learn from them. Amen.

commandments

God knows what is best for us, so he gave us special rules called commandments. These rules tell us how to love God and each other. For example, we are commanded to have a special day to worship God every week. And we must obey our parents. And we must not steal or lie.

This is what God said about his rules: "Learn them and be sure to obey them!" (Deuteronomy 5:1).

What is one of God's commandments?

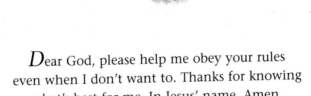

*D*ear God, please help me obey your rules
even when I don't want to. Thanks for knowing
what's best for me. In Jesus' name. Amen.

promises

When people make a promise, it means that they will do what they say. The Bible tells about God's promises to us. God promises to help us if we obey him. He promises to give us everything we need. He promises never to leave us.

Sometimes it's hard for people to do what they say. But God always keeps his promises. The Bible says: "You have done many good things for me, Lord, just as you promised" (Psalm 119:65).

Who always keeps his promises?

*D*ear Lord, thank you for keeping all
of your promises. Amen.

stories

There are many, many stories in the Bible. They all teach what is true. Some of them are about God's people. The stories tell about the good and bad things the people did. They tell how God was kind to his people and helped them. Some of the stories are about Jesus and the things he did.

Pretend stories are fun. But the stories in the Bible are even better! They are true, and they teach us about God.

Tell one of your favourite Bible stories.

*T*hank you, Lord, for true stories about Noah
and David and Esther and Jesus, and all the others.
I love to learn from Bible stories. Amen.

Psalms *(sahms)*

One book in the Bible is the book of Psalms.
The Psalms are songs and poems about God
and how he helps us. They remind us to thank
God for being so great and good. King David
loved God very much and wrote many of the
Psalms.

Ask someone to help you read Psalm 23 in
your Bible. You'll learn that David said God
was his shepherd.

A shepherd takes care of sheep. You can thank
God for taking good care of you the way a
shepherd cares for sheep.

*D*ear God, I love you. You are so big
and powerful, and you take good care of me.
Thank you! Amen.

prophecy *(prof-us-ee)*

A prophecy is a message about what is going to happen. Only God knows what is going to happen, so he gave messages of prophecy to Bible people called prophets. Long before Jesus was born, prophets wrote in the Bible that he was coming to live on the earth!

We don't know what will happen tomorrow or the next day. But God knows, so we don't have to worry about it!

Who helped each prophet know what to write?

*D*ear heavenly Father, thank you for telling us
what you want us to know and when you
want us to know it! Amen.

Gospels

The word gospel means "good news." Four books in the Bible are called the Gospels. They tell the good news about Jesus. The Gospels were written by four men. Their names were Matthew, Mark, Luke, and John.

Jesus loves children. That's good news! You can read about his love in the Gospels (Mark 10:13-16).

*D*ear God, the Bible says that Jesus loves me.
That's very good news! Thank you. Amen.

letters

People write letters to friends who live far away. The Bible has letters in it written by people who loved Jesus. God told them what to write. They sent the letters to people in churches far away. Then the people knew what God wanted them to do.

When we get a letter, we feel special. It means someone took the time to write to us. God thinks we're very special. There are many letters for us to read in the Bible.

Ask someone to help you read what Paul wrote in a letter to his friends (Ephesians 4:32).

*D*ear God, thank you for the letters that
Bible people wrote. I'm glad you wanted the letters
to be in the Bible. I pray in Jesus' name. Amen.

Old Testament

The first part of the Bible is called the Old Testament. It was written before Jesus was born. The Old Testament has a lot of stories about such people as Noah, Abraham, Joseph, Moses, Ruth, and King David.

When we read the Old Testament, we learn about many things that happened to God's people. We can read psalms and books of prophecy, too.

Was the Old Testament written before or after Jesus was born?

*L*ord, thank you for all of your Bible.
Thank you for all of the things
I can learn from it. Amen.

New Testament

The second part of the Bible is called the New Testament. It was written after Jesus was born. The New Testament has stories about Jesus in it. There are also stories about people who loved Jesus, such as Peter and John. And there are letters from people like Paul.

The New Testament is a very special part of the Bible. We can learn all about Jesus from the stories and letters there.

Was the New Testament written before or after Jesus was born? When was the Old Testament written?

*T*hanks, God, for the New Testament.
I'm glad I can learn about your Son, Jesus,
in this part of my Bible. Amen.

41

God
& People

Who is God?

Creator

A creator makes or creates things. God was the Creator of the sky and the sun, moon, and stars. He was the Creator of the world and people, too. Only God could make things as wonderful as that!

We like to make things out of clay. But God made our world out of nothing. After he made the world, he looked down upon it and liked it. He saw that it was good (Genesis 1:18).

Why is God called the Creator?

*D*ear God, you are so special. Only you could make something as big as the sun in the sky. And you keep it from falling down. Thank you! Amen.

heavenly Father

We call God our heavenly Father because he lives in heaven. Why is he our Father? It is because he gives us life. He gives us a special kind of life that will last forever. He does this because of his Son, Jesus. Our heavenly Father loves us even more than our fathers and mothers do. He takes care of us and helps us. He tells us we can be part of his family.

What are some ways the people in your family show that they love you? Who loves you even more than your mother and father?

Dear heavenly Father, I know my mum and dad
love me a lot. It's hard to understand how you
could love me more than that, but you do!
Thank you! Amen.

God
& People

Words that tell us
about God?

good

If someone is not bad, he is good. No one but God is always good. God does only what is good and right. He is very kind to us. He gives us everything we need. He gives us a beautiful world to enjoy. He gives us clothes and food, and he gives us our families.

We know that God is good because he does good things. We also know that "only God is truly good" (Mark 10:18). The Bible tells us so!

Who is always good?

*D*ear God, thank you for being so good to us.
You gave us our world, and you help us live in it
every day. You are good. Thank you! Amen.

loving

God is loving. That means he loves you. He loves you so much that he sent Jesus to be your friend. He feels sad when you forget to tell him that you love him, but he still loves you anyway.

This is how you can know that God loves you: The Bible says that God is love (1 John 4:8).

📖 Let's pray a little prayer now. Will you tell God that you love him?

*D*ear God, sometimes I forget to say that I love you.
I don't want you to feel sad. So I'll tell you right now,
"I love you, dear God!" I pray in Jesus' name. Amen.

powerful

Someone who is powerful can make things happen. No one is as powerful as God. He made billions of stars and keeps them from running into each other. He can stop storms and make sick people well, like the boy in the picture. He can hear all of our prayers at the same time.

Superman and Power Rangers look powerful, but they're not even real! God's power is real. He can do anything.

What powerful things can God do?

*L*ord, I feel safe when I remember how powerful you are. Help me remember your power whenever I'm scared. Thank you. Amen.

holy

God is holy. That means he never does anything wrong. He never sins. He is perfect. No one but God is holy. We should close our eyes and quietly think about how wonderful God is.

After you open your eyes, you can keep on thinking about how wonderful God is. You can even think about him when you run and jump!

What will you remember when you think about our holy God?

*T*hank you, God, for always doing what is right.
Thank you for loving me even though I'm not perfect
like you. In Jesus' name. Amen.

wise

A wise person knows about many things. Only God knows about everything. No one is as wise as God. He knows everything you have ever done, good or bad. He knows what you will do tomorrow. He knows how to answer your prayers.

God knows about everything, so he always knows what to do. That makes us feel very safe.

God is very wise. Does he know how good the boy in the picture is to his little brother?

Dear God, you know who I am,
and you know what I need.
Thank you for being so wise. Amen.

everywhere

God is everywhere. He is with you. He is at your friend's house. He is in heaven. And he is everywhere else. God is in every place there is, all at the same time.

We can't really understand how God can be everywhere. But we can believe his promise. He said, "I will be with you, and I will protect you wherever you go" (Genesis 28:15).

When you play hide-and-seek next time, thank God for being with you everywhere!

*D*ear God, I'm glad you are with me everywhere I go!
Thanks for protecting me. Amen.

God
& People

God's creation

earth

The earth is the place where all of us live. Another name for the earth is the "world." God, the Creator, made the world from nothing. He put water on the earth. In some places, he put dry land.

God had a good plan when he made our earth. He knew we needed land for growing food. And he knew we needed water for drinking and washing. He knows everything!

Who made the earth?

*L*ord, thank you for the earth you made for us.
Help us to take good care of it. Amen.

sky

The sky is what we see when we are outside and look up. God created the sky, and he created everything in it. He made the clouds and the sunshine. He made the stars and the moon.

The Bible says that when people look at the sun and moon and the stars in the sky, they know how wonderful God really is (Psalm 19:1-2).

When you look up at the sky at night, what can you see that God made?

*D*ear God, you are good! Thank you
for the big blue sky you made for our world.
I pray in Jesus' name. Amen.

plants

Plants grow in the ground that God put on the earth. God created many kinds of plants. He made big trees. He made little bushes. He made grass. He made beautiful flowers, like roses and violets.

When God made plants, it was like giving the world a big, soft cover. That cover is green, and it's beautiful!

Would you like to draw a picture of some of the pretty plants God made?

*F*ather, thank you for thinking of everything
when you made our world. Today I thank you
for all the plants you made for us. Amen.

fish

Fish swim in the water. God created the fish.
He made little fish and big fish. He made hundreds of kinds of fish. Some swim in long,
muddy rivers. Some swim in big round lakes.
And some swim in the huge oceans.
We like to swim and play in the water. But
we're different from fish. God planned for
them to live in the water, and they are happy
there.

Use your arms and pretend to swim like a fish
that God made.

*T*hanks, Lord, for the tiny little fish and
the great big whales and all of the fish in between!
In Jesus' name. Amen.

birds

Birds have feathers and wings. God created the birds and gave them songs to sing. He made the robins and the sparrows. He made the crows and the bluebirds and the canaries. He made the ducks and the geese.

The Bible says that God takes care of the birds. He feeds them (Matthew 6:26).

How many kinds of birds can you see in the picture? What colours do you see? Listen! Can you hear any birds singing outdoors?

*D*ear Lord, thank you for taking care of the birds
and for taking care of me. Amen.

animals

Animals live on the land God made. God created the animals. He made the dogs and cats and horses and cows. He made hundreds of different animals.

Think about the different places that God made for animals to live. Name an animal that lives in the woods. Name one that lives near your house. How many different animals can you name? How many animal sounds can you make?

*D*ear God, thank you for all the animals you made
for our world. I especially want to thank you
for [a pet or a favourite animal]. Amen.

people

Men and women and children are people. God created people. The first people he created were a man whose name was Adam and a woman whose name was Eve. He made them so they could talk to him and enjoy him. God loves all of the people he made. That means he loves you and me. He wants us to obey him so he can call us his friends (John 15:14).

Who were the first people God created?

*D*ear God, I'm glad that you decided to make people. Thank you for making me! Amen.

Garden of Eden

God gave Adam and Eve a beautiful place to live called the Garden of Eden. God said to take care of the Garden and enjoy it. But there was one fruit he said not to eat. Adam and Eve ate it anyway. God had to punish them for not obeying. Part of their punishment was that God sent them away. They couldn't live in the Garden of Eden any more.

The Garden was a happy place until Adam and Eve disobeyed God. Then they felt sad and afraid.

Where did Adam and Eve live before they disobeyed God?

Dear God, I wish that I always obeyed you.
But I know that I don't. Help me to always do
what you want me to do. Amen.

good

God is good. Everything God created was good, too. That means nothing was bad. The world was good, and everything God put in the world was good. But the people God made began to do bad things. In the picture, Cain is angry with his brother. That was not good. What is something good you do? What is something bad? You can ask God to help you be good. That will please him.

In the picture, what is happening? Is this right or wrong?

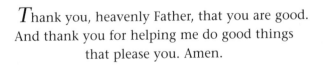

*T*hank you, heavenly Father, that you are good.
And thank you for helping me do good things
that please you. Amen.

Angels

Good and bad angels

angels

God made many special helpers called angels.
God sent an angel to protect Daniel in a den
of lions. Angels came to tell shepherds that
Jesus had been born. We can't see angels, but
God can send them to help us. There might be
angels here now, smiling at you.
Sometimes God sends angels to take care of us
even when we don't know about it.

Why did God send an angel to a lions' den?

*D*ear God, thank you for your angels.
Thank you for all your kindness to us. Amen.

Satan

One of the greatest angels, whose name is
Satan, turned against God. Another name for
Satan is the Devil. He made himself look like a
beautiful snake in the Garden of Eden. He got
Adam and Eve to disobey God.

When Satan turned against God, some other
angels went with him. These bad angels are
called demons. Satan and his demons try to
turn us against God, too. We must ask God to
protect us from Satan. Then Satan won't be
able to make us do wrong.

Is Satan a good angel or a bad angel?

*D*ear Lord, please help me to turn away
from Satan and his bad ideas. I love you, dear God,
and I want to obey you. In Jesus' name. Amen.

Jesus
&
Salvation

Who is Jesus?

Jesus

Jesus is God's only Son. A long time ago Jesus came to live on earth. He came from heaven. Jesus' mother was Mary, and Joseph took care of him like a father. But Jesus' real father is God. Jesus is God's Son.

Aren't you glad that Jesus lived on earth for a while? We can learn all about him from the Bible. Now he lives in heaven again and hears our prayers!

What is the name of God's Son?

*D*ear God, thank you for sharing your only Son,
Jesus, with us. In his name we pray. Amen.

Saviour

The name *Jesus* means "Saviour." A saviour saves people. Jesus saw that people were not obeying God. So Jesus came to save us from being punished by God. Jesus loves us so much that he died on the cross to take away our sins and be our Saviour.

Isn't it wonderful that Jesus came to be our Saviour? The Bible tells us, "Believe on the Lord Jesus and you will be saved" (Acts 16:31).

Why did Jesus want to be our Saviour?

Dear God, I know I've done wrong things.
Thank you for sending Jesus to be my Saviour.
In his name I pray. Amen.

Lord

A lord is in charge of other people. Jesus is our Lord. He wants to lead us and give us help. He is a loving and kind Lord. He can make you happy if you obey him. Always obey your Lord by doing what is right.

While you are growing up, your mum and dad are your guides. God has given them this job. Guess who is their guide. Jesus! He is in charge of them—and you!

Who is in charge of you? (Who is your Lord?)

*L*ord Jesus, thanks for being in charge.
Thanks for knowing what's best for me.
Help me to obey you. Amen.

Teacher

Teachers help us learn things. They teach us what they know. Jesus is the best teacher of all. He knows everything! We learn from Jesus by listening to Bible stories he told.

Would you like to hear one of the stories that Jesus told? Ask your mum or dad to read one of these stories to you from the Bible: The Good Samaritan (Luke 10:30-37) or A Lost Sheep (Luke 15:3-7).

*T*hank you, our Father in heaven, for sending Jesus
to our world to teach us how to live. Amen.

Jesus
&
Salvation

Jesus' birth

shepherds

People who take care of sheep are called shepherds. There were shepherds out in the fields on the night when Jesus was born. They were watching their sheep. Angels filled the sky and told them God's Son was born, and the shepherds were very happy.

Shepherds usually spend quiet nights with their sheep. The night when Jesus was born must have been the most exciting night of their lives!

How do you think the shepherds felt when angels told them Jesus was born?

*D*ear God, please help me to be excited about Jesus,
just like the shepherds were on the night
when Jesus was born. Amen.

Bethlehem

Angels told the shepherds that Jesus was born in the town of Bethlehem. The shepherds ran into town to find the baby.

An Old Testament prophet said that Jesus would be born in Bethlehem (Micah 5:2). He told about it a long time before Jesus came.

Can you say the name of the town where Jesus was born?

*D*ear God, thank you for sending your Son, Jesus,
to be born in the little town of Bethlehem,
just as the prophet said. Amen.

stable

Jesus was born in a stable. This place was like a barn, where cows and sheep live. What a strange place for God's Son to be born! Jesus left heaven to be born as a baby in a stable. The stable wasn't a fancy place. Anyone could go to see Jesus there. That's how God wanted it. He sent Jesus so that he could grow up and help everyone.

What is a stable?

*D*ear God, thank you for letting your Son, Jesus,
be born in a stable. I'm glad that he wants
to be everyone's friend. Amen.

manger

Baby Jesus did not have a crib. He slept in a manger. This was a box from which cows and sheep ate their hay. Mary and Joseph probably filled the manger with hay to make a soft bed for the baby Jesus.

Most babies sleep in little cribs with cuddly stuffed animals. But the baby Jesus slept in a box that cows and donkeys ate from. What a strange bed for God's Son!

Do you know the song "Away in a Manger"? Would you like to sing it now?

*D*ear God, thank you for giving baby Jesus
a special place to sleep. Thank you for taking care
of me, too. In Jesus' name. Amen.

wise men

Someone who is wise knows many things. When Jesus was born, some wise men from far away saw a star. They knew it was a special star. The wise men rode across the desert. They probably rode on camels. They followed the star and found Jesus! They gave him gifts.

People often travel a long way to see a new baby in the family. But there has never been a baby as special as Jesus. The wise men knew that. They worshipped him (Matthew 2:11).

What are some things the wise men did?

*D*ear Lord, those wise men in the Bible knew
that Jesus was the King. Help me to be wise, too.
Help me to accept Jesus, the Son of God,
as my own Saviour and King. Amen.

Jesus
&
Salvation

Jesus' life

Nazareth

Jesus grew up in the town of Nazareth. He lived with his mother, Mary, and with her husband, Joseph. Joseph was a carpenter, so Jesus helped him make things from wood. Jesus probably went to school in the town of Nazareth.

Jesus was a baby; then he crawled, walked, ran, and grew tall, just as you are doing.

Jesus' father is God in heaven. So who took care of Jesus when he was growing up in Nazareth?

*T*hank you, Lord, for Jesus' family and for his home. Thank you for my family and for giving me a home, too. In Jesus' name. Amen.

synagogue *(SIN-uh-gog)*

A synagogue was like a church building. It was also like a school. Jesus went there to pray. And he probably learned to read at the synagogue in Nazareth.

We go to church, and we go to school, too. We pray, and we learn many things. We can also pray right here and now.

What did Jesus do at a synagogue?

Dear God, I'm glad I can worship you
at my church. Help me to listen to the pastor
and to learn about you. Amen.

Temple *(TEM-pul)*

The Temple was like a big, beautiful church building. It was a very special place to worship God. Everyone who loved God went to the Temple at least once every year. Jesus went to the Temple with Mary and Joseph when he was twelve years old.

People who love God want to show it by what they do. Jesus and his family went to the big Temple to show God that they loved him.

When did Jesus first go to the Temple? Where do you go to show love for God?

*L*ord, help me to show others that
I love you by what I do and where I go.
I ask this in Jesus' name. Amen.

Jerusalem *(jeh-ROO-suh-lem)*

Jerusalem was a big city. It was an important city. That's where the Temple was. God's people came to Jerusalem from many different places. They came to worship God there. Jesus visited Jerusalem many times.

Exciting things happened in Jerusalem. The Bible says, "Every year Jesus' parents went to Jerusalem for the Passover festival" (Luke 2:41).

Can you say the name of the city where God's Temple was?

Lord, thanks for loving me wherever I live
and wherever I go! I love you, Lord. Amen.

miracles (MEER-uh-culs)

Because Jesus is God's Son, he did many wonderful things. We call these things miracles. Jesus made sick people well just by saying, "Be well." He made blind men's eyes see. He told a bad storm to stop, and it did. God gave his Son, Jesus, power to do these miracles.

The Bible tells us about Jesus' miracles. The things the Bible tells about really happened. So Jesus' miracles are real!

What are some miracles that Jesus did?

*T*hank you, Jesus, for the wonderful things
you can do because you are God's Son.
Nothing is too hard for you! I love you. Amen.

Good Shepherd

Jesus said, "I am the good shepherd." Shep-herds help their sheep find grass to eat and water to drink. They protect their sheep from wild animals. Jesus is our good shepherd. He helps us have food, and he protects us from harm.

When you go somewhere with your mum, you probably like to know that she is nearby. Your good shepherd is always near you.

 Pretend you are a sheep. Have a "shepherd" look for you and find you.

*J*esus, thank you for always watching over me.
You make me feel safe and loved, just like
a little sheep with his shepherd. Amen.

disciples *(dih-SIGH-puls)*

Jesus chose twelve men to be his special helpers. They were called Jesus' disciples. You may know some of their names: Peter, Andrew, James, John, Matthew. The disciples followed Jesus and learned from him. Then they told other people about Jesus.

You can't follow Jesus in the same way his twelve disciples did. But you can learn from him by listening to Bible stories. And you can help him by telling other people about him.

What did Jesus' disciples do?

*D*ear Jesus, I want to be your friend.
Help me to learn from you and tell
other people about you. Amen.

example

Jesus came to be an example for us. That means Jesus came to show us how to live. He is our example. The Bible tells us that Jesus loves people and helps them. He cares about people and is kind to them. We should try to be like Jesus.

Have you taken any kind of lessons—like swimming lessons or piano lessons? The teacher shows you just what to do, and you follow your teacher's example. Jesus is our teacher, too. He is our example.

How can we follow Jesus' example?

Dear Jesus, thank you for coming to earth
and showing us how to live. Help me
to love people just as you do. Amen.

Jesus
&
Salvation

Jesus' death

cross

Some bad people nailed Jesus to a cross made from two big pieces of wood. Jesus let them do it. He died on the cross to save us from our sins. Jesus never did anything wrong. But he died to take the blame for your sins and the sins of everyone in the world.

It's sad when people die. Do you know anyone who has died? People cried when Jesus was hurt and died on the cross. God, his Father, let him die for our sins because he loves us so much.

Why did Jesus die on the cross?

*D*ear Jesus, it makes me sad to think that you had to die on a cross. But I'm glad that you loved me enough to take away my sins. Amen.

tomb *(toom)*

Sometimes people are put in a tomb after they die. A Bible-time tomb was often a cave or hole in the side of a hill. Men put Jesus' body in a tomb after he died on the cross.

Jesus' friends put spices on his body (John 19:40). Then they put him in the tomb. They rolled a huge stone in front of it. But when Jesus came back to life again, not even a big stone could keep him inside!

Where did Jesus' friends put his body after he died?

*D*ear God, I'm glad that I didn't have to see Jesus' body put in a tomb. I'm glad that I know the happy ending to the story. God brought Jesus back to life again! Amen.

Jesus
&
Salvation

After Jesus' death

alive

The bad news is that Jesus died. The good news is that he did not stay dead. On the third day, God made Jesus become alive again. He walked and talked and ate with his friends. We can be his friends, too! Jesus lives! He is alive! He is in heaven with God, his Father.

Isn't it exciting to know that Jesus' body is no longer in a tomb? Angels said, "He isn't here! He has risen from the dead!" (Luke 24:6).

 Are you happy that Jesus is alive? Show it by singing or clapping your hands.

*D*ear Jesus, I'm so happy that you came back to life.
I love you, Jesus. Amen.

heaven

After Jesus died and became alive again, he
went back to heaven. It is a beautiful place.
No one there ever feels sad or gets sick or dies.
Jesus is getting a place ready in heaven for all
who love him. If you love Jesus, you will be
with him in heaven some day.
Name some fun places where you have been.
Heaven is better than any of those places! No
one ever cries there. Everyone is always happy!

Draw a picture to show how beautiful you think
heaven is.

Dear Lord, thank you for getting
heaven ready for us. What a wonderful place
to live forever with you! Amen.

return

To return means to come back. One day Jesus will leave his home in heaven and return to this earth. He will gather together all his friends. He will take us to live in heaven with him.

We know this is true because Jesus made a special promise: "When everything is ready, I will come and get you, so that you will always be with me where I am" (John 14:3). We don't know when that will be. So we should love Jesus and be ready!

What will Jesus do when he returns?

*D*ear Lord Jesus, I'm happy because
I know you're coming back!
Help me to love you and to be ready. Amen.

Jesus
&
Salvation

What is salvation?

salvation *(sal-VAY-shun)*

Salvation means that our sins are forgiven.
Jesus died on the cross so that we can have
salvation. The gift of salvation makes it
possible for us to be a part of God's family. We
become God's children now and forever.
It's fun to open presents on your birthday or
at Christmas. But here's the best gift ever: God
saves you when you believe. "It is a gift from
God" (Ephesians 2:8).

Tell what happens when we accept the gift of
salvation.

*D*ear God, what a wonderful gift salvation is!
Thank you for offering it to everyone.
In Jesus' name. Amen.

save

God loved us so much that he sent his Son, Jesus, from heaven. Jesus came to save us from our sins. Our sins keep us away from God, who is perfect. We could never pay enough money to be saved. We could never do enough good things to be saved. So God sent Jesus as a free gift to save us.

We're glad when someone comes to save us from a fierce dog or from water that's too deep. How wonderful that God sent Jesus to save us from our sins!

Why did God send Jesus to save us?

Dear God, thank you for sending Jesus to save
me from punishment of my sins.
How wonderful it is to know Jesus! Amen.

evil

God is good, but Satan is evil. Satan does many evil, or bad, things. He wants people to do evil things, too. If God doesn't want you to do something, then you shouldn't do it. It would be a bad thing to do.

God knows that evil things will always be going on until we get to heaven. So he tells us in the Bible to "run from all these evil things" (1 Timothy 6:11).

Every day and every night you can ask God to help you know what's good and what's bad. And he will! He will help you do what pleases him.

*D*ear God, please help me to run from evil
and do the good things you want me to do.
I pray this in Jesus' name. Amen.

sin

Whenever we do something wrong, or evil, it's called sin. We sin when we don't obey God. Adam and Eve were the first people. They didn't obey God. They sinned. Everyone does wrong things called sins. This makes God very sad.

Remembering Bible verses helps to keep us from sinning (Psalm 119:11). How? It helps us know what God wants. And that helps us know how to obey him.

 When we do things that are wrong, does it make God sad? What makes him glad?

*D*ear God, I'm sorry that I make you sad
when I do wrong things. Please forgive my sins.
And help me want to obey you and make you glad.
I pray this in Jesus' name. Amen.

forgive

God is ready to forgive anyone who comes to him. That means he forgets about the bad things we have done, and he is not angry with us. Instead, he loves us and helps us. He forgives us because Jesus died for us.
The Bible says that God forgives all our sins (Psalm 103:3).

Does God forgive you when you do things that are wrong? Tell him thank you!

*D*ear God, I'm thankful that you forgive me
when I do wrong things. Please help me to obey you
more and more. In Jesus' name. Amen.

faith

God wants us to have faith. If we have faith in Jesus, we believe everything he says. We know that he is God's Son, that he loves us, and that he died to save us. God helps us have faith to believe everything he says in the Bible. Perhaps you know a person who always does what he says. If he says that he will catch you when you jump from a high place, you believe him. You have faith in him. Everyone should have faith in Jesus.

Does God want you to have faith in Jesus?

*D*ear God, thank you that faith in Jesus is a gift from you. All I need to do is ask you for it. I'm asking for it right now. I pray in Jesus' name. Amen.

eternal life *(ee-TUR-nul LIFE)*

Eternal is a word that means "forever." Jesus wants you to have eternal life. He wants you to have a wonderful life in heaven that will last forever. Even after you die, you can be alive forever in heaven. You can have eternal life because of Jesus.

There is a whole year between birthdays. Right now a year seems like a very long time. But we can live with Jesus forever. That's more years than we can even count!

How long does eternal life last?

*D*ear God, being alive forever in heaven will be wonderful. We'll be with Jesus! Thank you! Amen.

Jesus
&
Salvation

How can I become part of
God's family?

believe

I must believe in Jesus. If I believe something, it means I know it is true. God wants me to believe that Jesus is his Son. He wants me to know that Jesus died for my sins. I can believe these things are true and trust Jesus to take away my sins. Then I will be part of God's family, and I will live for him.

The boy in the picture is excited. The teacher said that Jesus died for everyone. The boy is raising his hand and saying, "I believe it!"

What does God want you to believe?

*T*hank you, God, for your Son, Jesus.
I believe in Jesus with all my heart. Amen.

sorry

I must be sorry for doing wrong. All of us do things that God does not want us to do. That makes God sad. He waits to hear each of us say, "I am sorry, God, for the wrong things I have done."

It's important to say you're sorry. It's also important to show it by not doing the same wrong things over and over again.

 Do you want to tell God you are sorry about something you did? He will forgive you and help you not do it again.

*D*ear God, when I do wrong things, help me to say,
"I'm sorry." In Jesus' name. Amen.

accept

When someone gives you a gift, you don't look the other way. You accept the gift. Jesus wants you to accept his gift of salvation. He will help you do what pleases him right now and all day tomorrow. And he will let you live with him in heaven one day.

People who give gifts are happy to watch us accept them and open them. Jesus is happy when we accept his gift to us, too.

Jesus wants you to accept his gift. Perhaps you would like to do this now. You can pray and tell him, "Yes, thank you, Jesus!"

*D*ear God, thank you for sending Jesus
to save me from sin. Thank you for your gift
to me of Jesus. Amen.

trust

I must trust Jesus. If I trust him, that means I believe that he is God's Son. I know for sure that he loves me and that he died on the cross for me. If I put my trust in Jesus, that means I know he cares for me and helps me to do what is right.

In the picture, Jeremy says that he doesn't think you can trust anyone. But his friend tells him, "You can trust Jesus!"

What does it mean to trust Jesus?

*D*ear Jesus, I believe that you are God's Son
and that you died for me. I'm glad that
I can trust you to help me. Amen.

The
Holy Spirit
&
Christian Living

Who is the Holy Spirit?

The Holy Spirit

When we ask Jesus to be our Saviour, the Holy Spirit comes to live within us. We cannot see the Holy Spirit, but he is always with us. These three persons are one God:

God the Father

God the Son (Jesus)

God the Holy Spirit

The mother in the picture is saying, "God the Holy Spirit is right here with us."

 You can say these words: "I believe in God the Father, God the Son, and God the Holy Spirit. These three are the one God who loves me."

*D*ear God, I'm glad the Holy Spirit is with me
wherever I go. In Jesus' name. Amen.

counsellor

A counsellor is wise. He can tell people the best thing to do. God the Holy Spirit is a special counsellor to everyone who loves Jesus. He is with us all the time. He shows us what is right and wrong.

The girl in the picture has a counsellor—the Holy Spirit. He helps her know it would be wrong to take a chocolate bar.

What can the Holy Spirit, your counsellor, show you?

*D*ear God, thank you for giving me the Holy Spirit
to help me decide what's the right thing to do. Amen.

Helper

God the Holy Spirit is my special helper. He has power to help me stand up against everything that's bad. When others do wrong things, the Holy Spirit helps me say, "No, I don't do things like that."

I must let the Holy Spirit be my helper. He helps me to do right and to help others. The Holy Spirit helps me to be strong about choosing what is right.

When do you need the Holy Spirit to be your helper?

*D*ear Lord, thank you for giving us the
Holy Spirit to be our helper. I'm glad I can
ask him for help to do what's right!

The
Holy Spirit
&
Christian Living

Ways I show that God's
Holy Spirit helps me

love

When you love someone, you care about that person very much and try to show how you feel. The Holy Spirit helps you show your love for God and for your family and for other people, too. He helps you show love by the words you say and by the way you act. The Bible tells us, "Let us stop just saying we love each other; let us really show it by our actions" (1 John 3:18).

How do you show your love for God?

*D*ear God, I need the Holy Spirit to help me
be more loving. Help me show love by the words
I say and by the way I act. Amen.

joy

Joy is a special happiness that comes from the Holy Spirit. It's better than being happy. You can be joyful even when you are sick because you know that God will take care of you. You can have joy even when you are alone because you know that God is always with you and will never leave you.

It may seem hard to be happy when you're sick. But the Holy Spirit will help you have more and more joy!

Can you have joy all the time? Why?

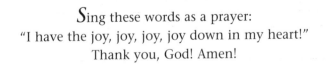

Sing these words as a prayer:
"I have the joy, joy, joy, joy down in my heart!"
Thank you, God! Amen!

peace

The Holy Spirit can help us have peace when we feel afraid. He helps us to know that he is with us all the time. We can have peace if we pray when it is dark or stormy or when we feel sick or sad. The Holy Spirit will help us not feel afraid. We'll have real peace.

The Bible says, "If the Holy Spirit controls your mind, there is life and peace" (Romans 8:6).

Act out not being afraid on a stormy night.

Dear God, I get scared during a storm.
Please give me peace from the Holy Spirit,
and remind me that you're always with me. Amen.

patience *(PAY-shuns)*

Patience is when you are willing to wait. Maybe you must wait for your turn or for others to finish what they are doing. God the Holy Spirit will help you have patience. He will help you not get upset when you have to wait.

Sometimes it's very hard to wait! But the Holy Spirit will help you be patient if you ask him. He will help you even if you have to wait for a very long time.

 Do you need to have patience with someone— a friend or a brother or sister? Who can help?

*L*ord, I pray that the Holy Spirit will give me patience whenever I begin to feel upset. Thank you for caring about me. In Jesus' name. Amen.

kindness

Kindness is when we are helpful and good. It's when we say nice things to our family and friends. We are kind when we share and when we do things that make people and animal friends happy.

Calling someone a mean name is not kind. Saying a friend can't play with your toys is not kind. God says, "Be kind to each other" (Ephesians 4:32).

How will you show kindness to a friend? Can you be kind to an animal, too?

Dear God, I like it when people are kind to me.
Help me to always be kind, just like you said.
In Jesus' name. Amen.

goodness

Goodness is when we do what is right and good. God is good. And when we obey him, we are good. We are good when we behave and do what our parents ask us to do. God gives us the Holy Spirit to help us know what is right and good to do.

It may not always be easy to be good. But God says, "Don't get tired of doing what is good" (Galatians 6:9).

Ask God to show you what is right and good to do.

*D*ear Lord, thank you for the Holy Spirit, who helps
me to choose what is good. In Jesus' name. Amen.

gentleness

Gentleness is when you are not rough with your pets or your friends or your baby sister or brother. Gentleness is when you are careful with your toys and put them away without breaking them. The Holy Spirit will help you to be gentle.

The Bible tells us we are to be gentle even in the way we talk (Proverbs 15:1).

Show how to be gentle with a stuffed toy.

*L*ord, help me to be gentle when I play.
Help me to talk in a gentle way, too. Amen.

The
Holy Spirit

&

Christian Living

Ways to please God
wherever I am

obey

To obey means to do what we are told to do.
It is important to obey God, who made us and
knows what is best for us. He tells us to love
him and to love other people. It is important
to obey parents and teachers, too, because
God wants us to do this. He knows it is best.
Your parents know what things could hurt
you. That's one reason why God wants you to
obey them. God knows what's best, so we
should always do what he wants.

Is it hard to obey? (Tell God—he will help you.)

*D*ear God, I want to obey, but sometimes
I just forget. Please help me do what is right.
In Jesus' name. Amen.

pray

When we pray, we are talking to God. He can always help us because he is great and powerful. God wants both children and grown-ups to pray to him. He wants us to talk to him. We can tell him anything, at any time, in any place.

It's fun to spend time with someone you like. God is happy when we spend time with him by praying (Proverbs 15:8).

Can you pray for someone just like the girl in the picture is praying for her mother? She is saying, "Please, God, help Mum feel better."

Dear God, I like to talk to you.
I want to tell you about _____ . Amen.

197

praise

We praise God when we tell him how great he is and how much we love him. We can praise God with the words we say when we pray. We can praise God with the songs we sing, too.

It makes you feel good when people tell you nice things, doesn't it? God likes to hear from you, too.

There is no one as wonderful as God. So it should be easy to praise him by telling him so! Praise him, praise him, all children of the world!

*T*hink about God and say, "Dear Father in heaven,
I praise you because you are so
wonderful and wise and powerful."

thank

We say thank you when we get a present or someone does something nice for us. When we pray, we can thank God for everything he gives us. We can also thank him for everything he does for us.

We should remember to thank God every day. The Bible says to "thank him for all he has done" (Philippians 4:6).

Would you like to do what the girl in the picture is doing? She is drawing things she wants to thank God for. You can also make a list of things for which you thank God. Name things and have someone write them for you.

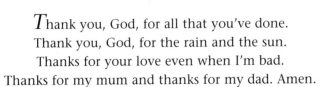

*T*hank you, God, for all that you've done.
Thank you, God, for the rain and the sun.
Thanks for your love even when I'm bad.
Thanks for my mum and thanks for my dad. Amen.

forgive

We must ask God to forgive us for the wrong
things we do and to help us to stop doing
them. Then he will forget about them. We
must also forgive others who do wrong things
to us. Then we can still be their friend. God
will help us.

God tells us in the Bible, "If you forgive
others, you will be forgiven" (Luke 6:37).

Is there something for which God should forgive
you? Who should you forgive?

*D*ear God, thank you for forgiving me for wrong
things I do. Help me to forgive my friends when they
do wrong things to me. In Jesus' name. Amen.

help

When we help people, we do what we can to make their work easier. Loving Jesus makes us want to help others. We can do our best to help at home without complaining or whining. Sometimes our friends need help, too. We show love for Jesus by being a helper. Your mum and dad are happy when you help at home. God is happy, too. He likes it when you help people at home, at school, or wherever you are.

Who can you help today or tomorrow?

I want to be a good helper, Lord.
I want to please you by helping someone
every day. Amen.

witness

A witness tells what he has seen or heard.
People who see accidents are called witnesses.
They are often asked to tell what they know.
You know a lot about Jesus. So you can be a
witness for Jesus by telling others about him.

Witness to your friends by letting them know
that Jesus loves them. One way to do that is to
show your friends your Bible storybooks.

Dear God, help me to tell my friends all about you.
Show me how to be a witness for you.
In Jesus' name. Amen.

The Church

Words about the church

church

People who love Jesus worship him. Some meet in big buildings or in homes or in other places. The place where we meet for worship is often called a church. God is happy when we go to church to learn about him and to worship him.

It doesn't matter where we meet. What's important is that we worship God.

Tell about the church where you worship.

*T*hank you for my church, Lord. I learn
about you there and have fun with my friends.
It's a very special place. Amen.

church

The real church is not a building. It is the group of people who belong to God's family. God is happy when the people in his family worship him together.

Do you have aunts, uncles, cousins, and grandparents? It's fun to have a family to enjoy. Our church family is like that. The Bible tells us that Jesus is the leader of the church family (Colossians 1:18).

Who do you know in your church family?

*T*hank you, God, for my church friends.
We love each other, and we all love you! Amen.

Christians

People who love Jesus are called Christians. The first part of this word is "Christ," which is another name for Jesus. Sometimes we use these two names together. We can say that we are Christians if we believe in Jesus Christ. Not everyone is a Christian. The Bible tells us that believing in Jesus is the way we become Christians.

Is believing in Jesus the only way to be a Christian?

Dear God, I believe that Jesus Christ is your Son.
I love him very much. Thank you that
I can be a Christian. Amen.

minister

The minister of a church explains the Bible to all of the people in the church family. The minister also visits people and prays for people who are sick. Sometimes a minister is called a pastor.

Do you know your minister's name? Does he know your name? Why not shake hands with him the next time you see him at church? You can tell him that you're praying for him, too.

Dear God, I'm glad you sent Minister_____
to our church. Please keep him strong and help him
teach us about you. In Jesus' name. Amen.

preach

To preach means to talk to people about Jesus.
It means to tell people how Jesus wants them
to live. It is important for everyone to know
that Jesus is God's Son and that he loves us. It
is important for people to know how to obey
Jesus. A minister preaches from the Bible to
help people know these things.

Anyone who preaches about Jesus is doing
what Jesus said to do. He said, "Preach the
Good News to everyone, everywhere"
(Mark 16:15).

What book does your minister use when he
preaches?

*D*ear God, thank you for everyone who preaches about Jesus. Thank you for ministers and missionaries all over the world. Amen.

leaders

Every church family has leaders. These church leaders are in charge of the work of the church. They teach the people to do what is right. They also help the people in the church who have special needs.

What would happen if your church had no leaders or teachers? no one to take food to people who need it? no one to take care of the church?

Ask your family to tell you who some of the leaders are at your church.

*T*hank you, God, for all of the leaders in my church.
Please help them to be good leaders. Amen.

The Church

Things we do at church

worship

When we worship God, we think about him and all he does for us. He gives us our families, our friends, and our best friend, Jesus. When we say, "I love you, Jesus," that is worship. It is good to worship God with our church family.

The Bible says, "Come, let us worship" (Psalm 95:6). We please God when we worship him.

Who is it that we think about when we worship God?

*D*ear God, I'm glad that I can worship you
with my church family. Amen.

prayers

One of the ways we worship God is by praying together. Our prayers are the words we say when we pray or talk to God. We can talk to God about everything. We can thank him and tell him we love him and ask him to help us. Praying with our church family is a special way to worship God. When we pray together, we "share each other's troubles and problems" (Galatians 6:2).

Who is it that we talk to when we say our prayers?

*D*ear God, I'm glad I can talk to you any time.
I'm also glad that I can say prayers
with other people who love Jesus. Amen.

sing

When we sing together, we make beautiful music with our voices. Sometimes people sing together in a choir (KWI-ur). We worship God when we sing about him and when we sing to him. He likes to hear our songs.

The Bible tells us to be happy when we sing to God. It says, "Come before him, singing with joy" (Psalm 100:2).

 Sing a favourite song about Jesus. Do you know the song "Jesus Loves Me"?

*D*ear Jesus, thank you for loving me. I love you, too.
Help me to love you more and more. Amen.

hymns *(hims)*

When everyone sings together at church, we often sing songs that are called hymns. The hymns we sing help us think about God. We worship God when we sing hymns together. We can sing hymns in other places, too. We can worship God by singing hymns any time and anywhere.

Some hymns were written by people who lived a long time ago. They loved Jesus and gave us songs we can still sing to him.

Do you like to sing hymns with other people who love Jesus?

*T*hank you, Lord, for the hymns we sing at church.
People have loved you for many, many years.
I love you now! In Jesus' name. Amen.

offering

At church we bring our offering money to God. We worship God when we give an offering. God gives us our families, food, homes, and everything we have. One way to thank God is to give some of our money for his work.

The Bible says that "God loves the person who gives cheerfully" (2 Corinthians 9:7).

What can you give to God? You can give him your love. Maybe you can also give food to poor people and give money for God's work.

*D*ear God, thank you for all you have given me. I'm glad that I can give you an offering to show you that I love you. Amen.

listen

We worship God when we use our ears to listen to the Bible. Children listen to Bible stories. They listen to teachers explain the words. Grown-ups and children listen when someone reads the Bible at church. They listen to the pastor explain the Bible.

How have grown-ups learned so much? They've listened! You can do that, too, especially in church. You can learn a lot from the Bible—if you listen.

Is there a Bible story you would like to listen to right now?

*L*ord, I like to wriggle and make noise. But please help me to be quiet and listen carefully to my teachers at Sunday school and church. Amen.

learn

We can learn about God and his Son, Jesus, at church. We learn by listening to the Bible. We learn by making things. We even learn by playing together. People who love Jesus can help each other learn to know all about him.

Who helps you learn about Jesus? Can you name something you made that helped you remember a Bible story? What helps you think about how Jesus wants you to act?

*D*ear God, help me to learn all about you from my
teacher, my pastor, and all of the leaders at church.
Thank you for them. Amen.

baptise

In Bible times, John the Baptist told people to be baptised. In this picture, John has just baptised Jesus in a river. Jesus told his disciples to baptise people. Jesus tells us to be baptised, too. Baptism lets others know that we belong to Jesus. Today, people are often baptised at church.

Ball players wear uniforms to let everyone know what team they're on. Being baptised is one way to let everyone know that we have chosen to follow Jesus.

What does our baptism let others know?

*D*ear Jesus, thank you that I can belong to you.
Thank you that I can show my love for you
by being baptised. Amen.

Lord's Supper

At church we have the Lord's Supper. In some churches it is called Communion. Those who love the Lord Jesus eat bread together and drink from a cup. That's what Jesus did with his disciples before he died on the cross. Maybe you have wondered why people eat and drink so little at the Lord's Supper. We don't eat this special meal because we are hungry. We eat it to remember that Jesus died for us.

What do we remember at the Lord's Supper?

*L*ord, I'm glad that we have Communion at my church. It helps me to think about your dying on the cross for me. Thank you for loving me so much. Amen.

fellowship *(FELL-oh-ship)*

People who love Jesus like to have fellowship together. That means they like to be together. They like to be good friends because they have the same best friend, Jesus. When Christians have fellowship, they often eat and have fun together.

After Jesus went back to heaven, his friends liked to be together. They "shared their meals with great joy" (Acts 2:46).

What fun things can Christian families do when they meet together?

*D*ear Lord, thank you for the fun times I have with the
people in my church family. They love me,
and I love them! I thank you in Jesus' name. Amen.

Alphabetical Index of Words

About the Authors

William O. Noller is international publishing director for Tyndale House Publishers. A graduate of Trinity Evangelical Divinity School, Bill has been involved in Christian education and Christian publishing for thirty-five years. He travels internationally, publishing Christian books in foreign languages throughout the world.

Bill resides in San Dimas, California, with his wife, Diana Lee. They have two grown children and three grandchildren.

Bill submitted the original manuscript for this book. It was his desire to help children around the world learn many of the key words of the Christian faith from the Bible. To accomplish this, Bill organised the book according to a simplified doctrinal outline. Bill's friend Ken Taylor helped to complete the manuscript. And Dr. William F. Kerr made valuable suggestions and recommendations.

Kenneth N. Taylor is best known as the writer of The Living Bible, which has been revised by a group of biblical scholars to become the New Living Translation. His first claim to fame, though, was as a writer of children's books. Ken and his wife, Margaret, have ten grown children and numerous grandchildren. Ken's early books were written for use in the family's daily devotions. The manuscripts were ready for publication only when they passed the scrutiny of ten young critics! Those books, which have been read to two generations of children around the world, include *The Living Bible Story Book* and *My Little Bible in Pictures*.

My First Bible Words is a companion to Ken Taylor's *My First Bible in Pictures*.